T0193180

My First Book About DNA

-Katie Woodard

To order additional copies of this book, contact:
Xlibris
844-714-8691
www.Xlibris.com
Orders@Xlibris.com

ISBN: Softcover   978-1-4010-7816-4

Library of Congress Control Number: 2002095088

Print information available on the last page

Rev. date: 11/17/2021

Did you know that you have DNA?

You do!
Everyone has DNA.
And DNA is so neat that
everyone's DNA is different,
just like every person
is different.

Just like every
snowflake is different!

What is DNA?
It stands for the long word
"DeoxyriboNucleic Acid,"
but everyone calls it by
its nickname, "DNA."

Your DNA is way too small
to see with just your eyes.
You have to use a special
microscope to see it.
Let's take a closer look!

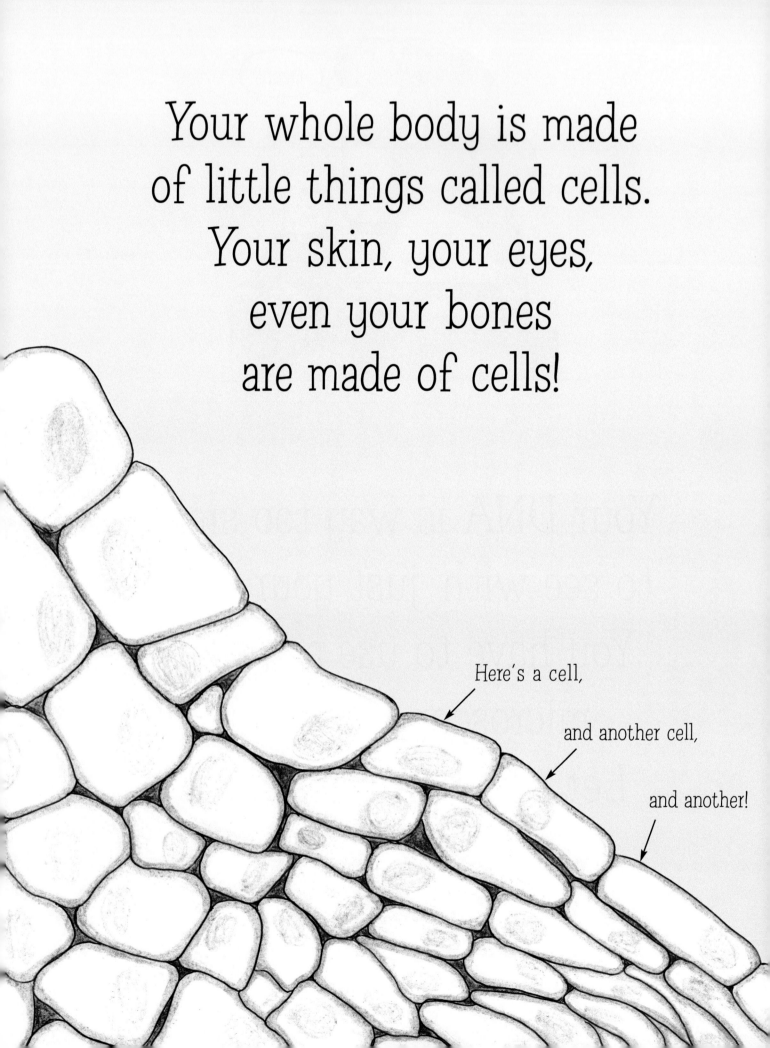

Your whole body is made
of little things called cells.
Your skin, your eyes,
even your bones
are made of cells!

Here's a cell,

and another cell,

and another!

Cells are VERY tiny.
There are 20 trillion cells that make up your body. That's thousands of times more than the number of people in the whole world!

That's a lot of cells!

All animals
are made of
cells too, and
so are plants!

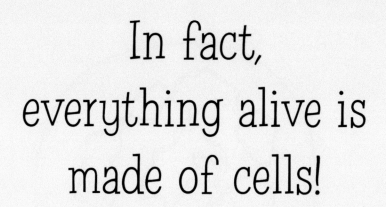

In fact,
everything alive is
made of cells!

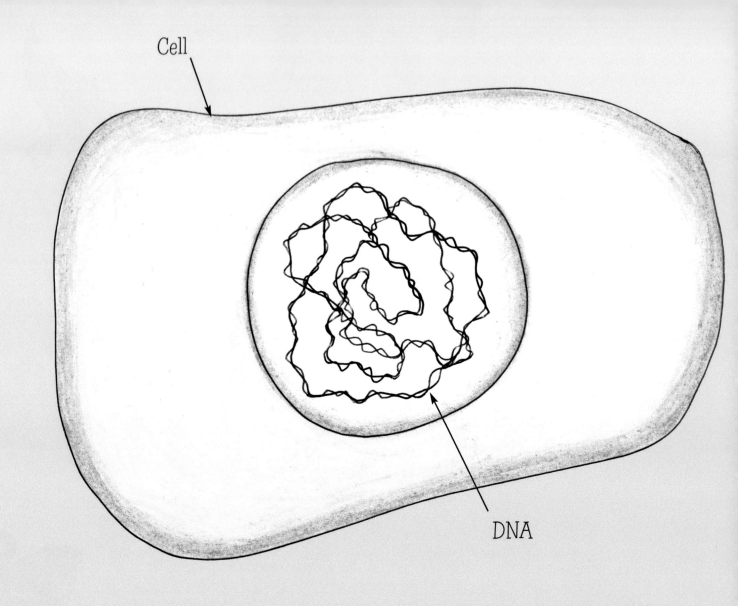

Cell

DNA

Inside a cell is something
called a nucleus.
Coiled up inside the nucleus
is DNA!

All the DNA in a cell is called a genome, because it is made up of smaller parts called genes.

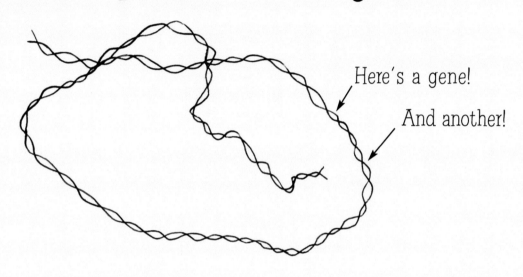

DNA is very, very tiny,
but very, very long.
If you put all of your DNA
together at the ends,
it would reach to the moon
and back 8 times!

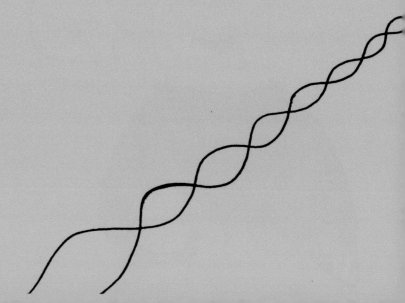

That's a lot
of DNA!

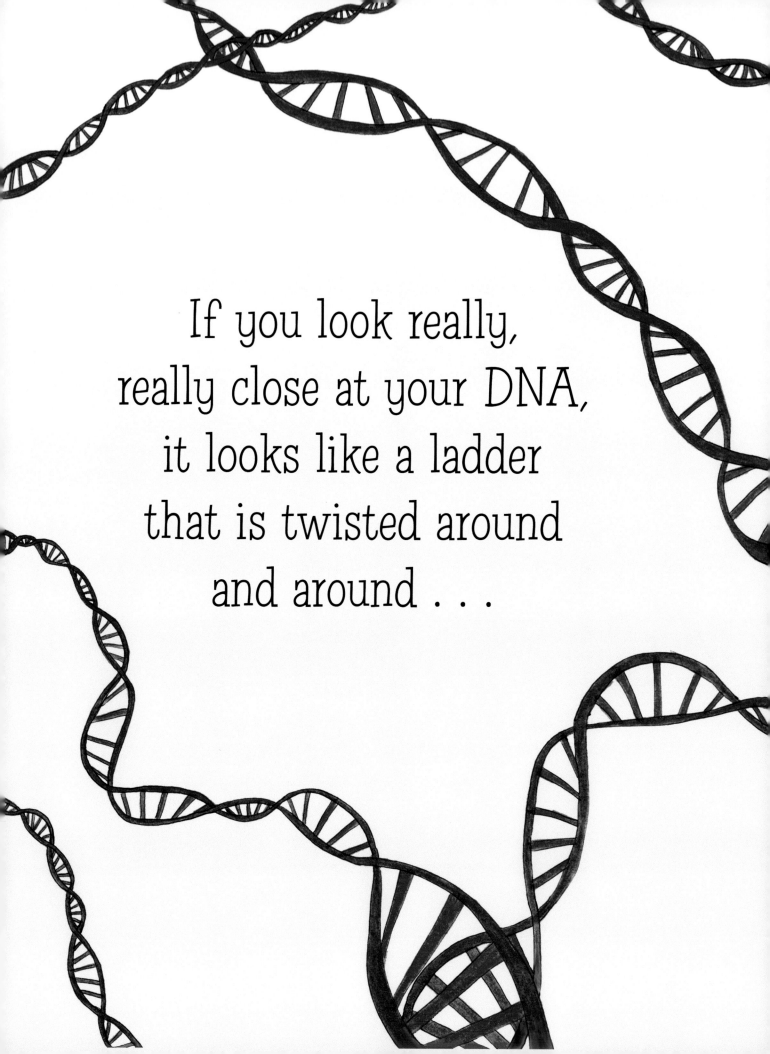

If you look really,
really close at your DNA,
it looks like a ladder
that is twisted around
and around . . .

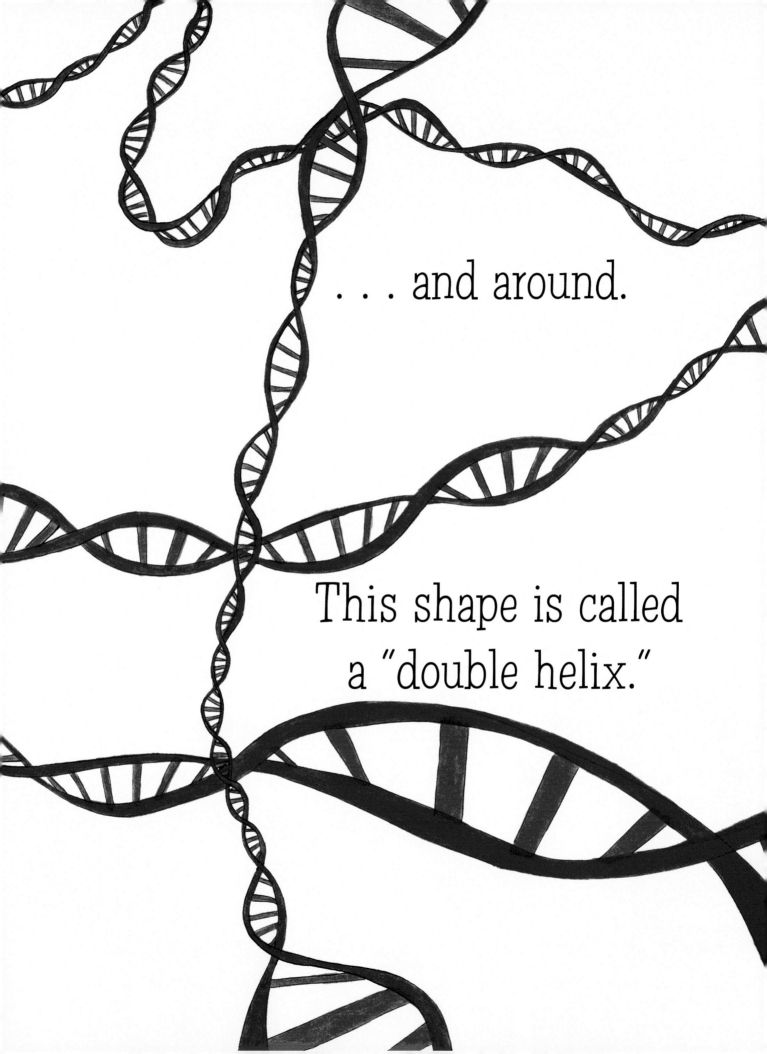

. . . and around.

This shape is called
a "double helix."

Your DNA has a code that is
like a recipe for you.
It says what color eyes, hair
and skin you have . . .

. . . whether you are short, tall, or in between. It even says what you are allergic to!

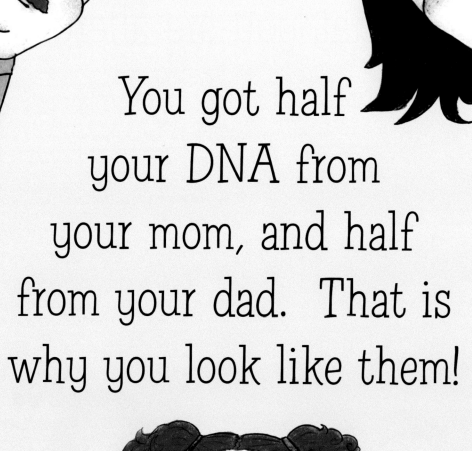

You got half
your DNA from
your mom, and half
from your dad. That is
why you look like them!

Your DNA is different than everyone else's in the whole world, unless you have a twin brother or sister.

Twins have matching DNA!

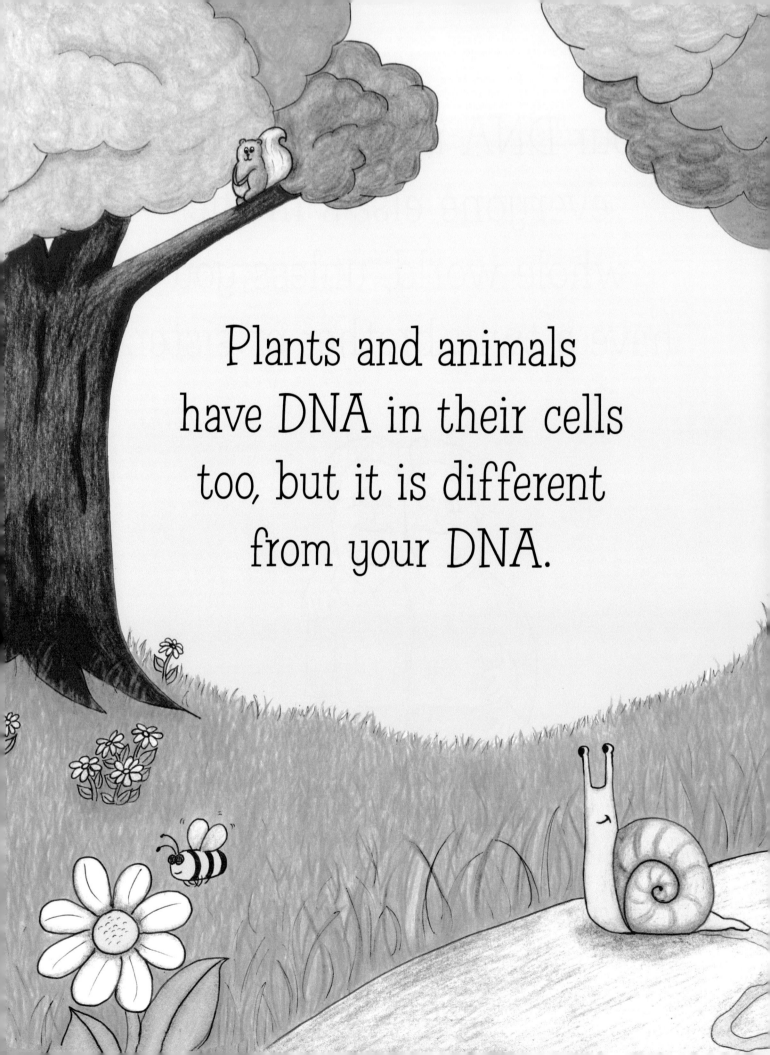

Plants and animals have DNA in their cells too, but it is different from your DNA.

That is why
you don't look
like them!

But why is DNA really so neat?
Because we can do a lot with DNA!
We can study DNA to learn about
how and why we get sick.

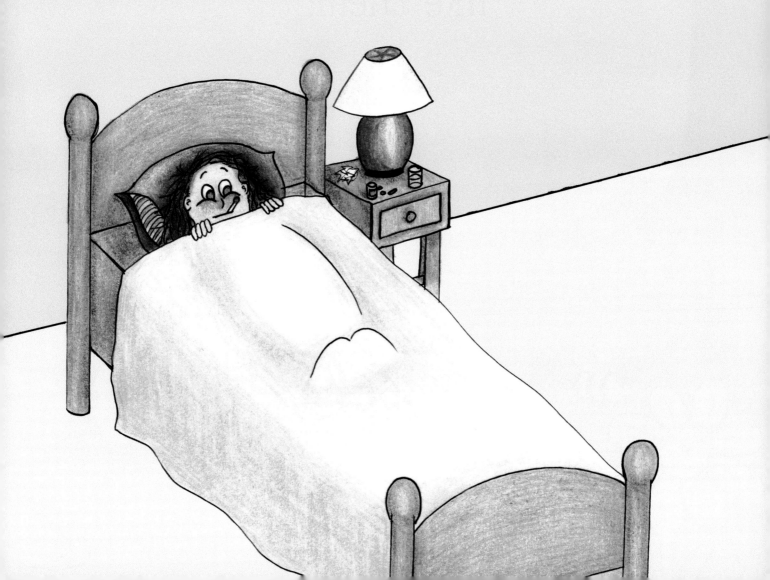

Then we can sometimes
cure people,

or keep them from
even getting sick!

We can use DNA to
catch criminals!
If a robber leaves a hair inside a
house, scientists can find out
whose DNA it has, and then
send the robber to jail.

Scientists can also get DNA from fingernails, tiny drops of blood, and spit!

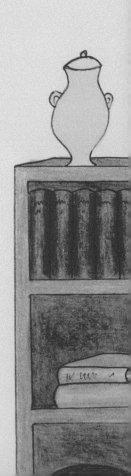

We can even use DNA to
clone things!
This means making an exact copy
of something using its DNA.
Scientists have cloned some
animals, but not people.

Now you know a lot about your DNA. Scientists learn more about DNA every day! Someday will you be a scientist who studies DNA?

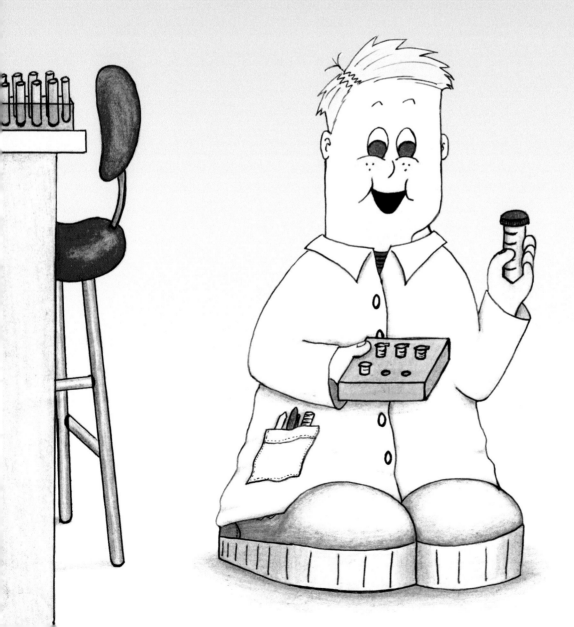

Printed in the United States
by Baker & Taylor Publisher Services